BEST DRESSED TABLES

Marie
Kurt

BEST DRESSED TABLES

Susan Hyatt

GRANVILLE ISLAND
PUBLISHING

Publisher's Cataloging-in-Publication Data

Names: Hyatt, Susan, 1950–, author
Title: Best dressed tables / Susan Hyatt.
Description: Includes bibliographical references. | Vancouver, BC: Granville Island Publishing, 2019.
Identifiers: ISBN 978-1-989467-05-3 (Hardcover) | 978-1-989467-06-0 (ebook)
Subjects: LCSH Table setting and decoration. | Food presentation.| Table etiquette. | Entertaining. | BISAC COOKING / Tablesetting | DESIGN / Decorative Arts
Classification: LCC TX879 .H93 2019 | DDC 642/.8—dc23

Book editor: Elspeth Richmond
Book designer: Omar Gallegos
Proofreader: Rebecca Coates

Granville Island Publishing Ltd.
212 – 1656 Duranleau St. Granville Island
Vancouver, BC, Canada V6H 3S4

604-688-0320 / 1-877-688-0320
info@granvilleislandpublishing.com
www.granvilleislandpublishing.com

Printed in Korea

Acknowledgements

I dedicate this book to my amazing parents who inspired me to be who I am today.

I love entertaining and setting tables. In *Best Dressed Tables* I wanted to share some of my ideas with you, to help you set beautiful tabletops in your home, enjoy doing it and be proud of the result.

It takes a village to write a book, and it wouldn't have been possible without my dear friend and part-time secretary, Sherri Slobodian, who supported my efforts from the very beginning, and photographic technician extraordinaire Sean Stephenson, for his amazing work. I also want to send a thank you to my daughter Jessica Gares from Kismet Communications, who has been a tremendous help.

Thanks also to my wonderful husband Martin and my children Lani, Shelley, John, and Jessica, along with my five beautiful grandchildren Melissa, Dylan, Liam, Johnny, and Oliver and my dear friends for their support and encouragement in this venture.

Working with Jo Blackmore and her dedicated team of Omar, Elspeth, Conni and Jeff has been a wonderful experience that I will forever treasure. Jo's guidance and brilliance when it comes to publishing is wonderful to see and Omar puts his soul into every part of the design. The editing process with Elspeth was so enjoyable and quite the process. Conni's eye for detail and enthusiasm and belief in me was very special. I certainly was made to feel a part of the Granville Island Publishing family.

Contents

ACKNOWLEDGEMENTS	v
INTRODUCTION	1
BRUNCHES	2
Morning Glory	4
Butterflies and Blueberries	6
My Love of Palms	8
Provence	10
Sassy Flamingos	12
Androsia and Starfish	14
Beach House in Qualicum	16
Moroccan Flair	18
French Country	20
Reading Room	22
LUNCHEONS	24
Spring Has Sprung	26
Shades of Blue	28
Ladies' Luncheon by the Pool	30
Summer Stripes by the Sea	32
Working Lunch	34
Understated Elegance	36
Tumbling Seashells	38
Red Poppies Delight	40
Birds of a Feather	42
Red Coral and Seashells on the Terrace	44
Flirty Flamingos	46
All Aboard	48
She Sells Seashells	50
Luncheon by the Lake	52
Family Barbecue	54
Anchors Aweigh	56
Hibiscus and Bougainvillea	58
Apple of My Eye	60
Caribbean Influence	62
Ladies Who Lunch	64
Mellow Yellow	66
Artichokes, Anyone?	68
Lunch on a Bench	70
DINNER PARTIES	72
West Coast Vibes	74
Fine Dining	76
Boats and Bridges	78
All About Coral	80
Festive Fruits and Veggies	82
Early Dinner by the Ocean	84
Leaves Everywhere	86
Romance in the Air	88
Splendour in the Summer	90
Inspired by Citrus	92
Crisp Green and White	94
White Linen and Orchids	96
Shades of White	98

Versailles 100
Black and White 102
Condo Dinner 104
Greek Chic 106
Tortoiseshell and Tangerine 108
Key Lime and Silver 110
Tahitian 112
Parrots and Tropical Leaves 114
Al Fresco 116

GET TOGETHERS 118

Purple Haze 120
Coffee with a View 122
Young Ladies at Tea 124
Tea Time 126
Tea for Two 128
Fall Picnic 130
Happy Hour 132
Cocktails at the Bar 134

CELEBRATIONS 136

Birthdays
- Seashells and Flowers 138
- Tropical Fruits and Exotic Florals 140
- Pink and Blue 142

Valentine's
- X's and O's 144
- Be Mine 146
- Love Is Red 148
- The Shape of My Heart 150

Easter
- Pastels and Tulips 152
- All About Bunnies 154
- Yellows and Greens 156
- Stripes and Ribbons 158

Thanksgiving
- All About Pumpkins 160
- Harvest Glory 162

Christmas
- Christmas Plaid 164
- Santa Claus Is Coming to Town 166
- Christmas for Two 168
- Golden Hues 170
- All That Glitters 172

New Year's
- Starry New Year's Eve 174
- Hello, Gorgeous 176
- A Golden Touch 178
- Snowy Day 180

TRAVELLING TABLES 182

Italy: Renaissance 184
Greece: Santorini Blue 190
Turkey: Good Morning 194
United States: Modern Elegance 200
Bahamas: Bahamian Rhapsody 204
Maui: Tropical Vibrations 210

TIPS AND SUGGESTIONS 216

SOURCES 227

RECIPE CREDITS 229

PHOTO CREDITS 231

Introduction

For over twenty-five years, I pioneered destination wedding planning, taking great pleasure in custom designing the perfect wedding for couples and their guests in the Bahamas, Hawaiian Islands and Puerto Vallarta as well as here in Vancouver.

My passion for event planning — and entertaining — naturally dovetailed into setting beautiful tables for all occasions. I believe an attractive and creative table sets the tone for a memorable occasion, while making every guest feel special and welcome. I also love sharing my ideas and inspiring others to get creative. So, with the support of my family and friends, I decided to write *Best Dressed Tables* to showcase some of my favourite tables while encouraging you to create your own tabletops.

When I'm hosting a brunch, luncheon or dinner party, I often aim to transport my guests around the world by just taking a seat at my table — and you can too. In the *Tips and Suggestions* section, I show you how to create settings simply, enjoyably and affordably. I also take my love for entertaining on the road when I travel; the *Travelling Tables* section showcases settings that I styled during my travels. You will also find a few special recipes that I enjoy and hope you will too.

Brunches

Brunch is a favourite with everyone, whether it's a formal affair or a casual gathering with family and friends.

Morning Glory

The beautiful centrepiece I received from the Margaret Trudeau evening in Vancouver, where she was talking about her book *Changing My Mind*, inspired this breakfast table. Oranges and yellows awaken the senses and complement the lovely fresh arrangement.

Butterflies and Blueberries

I used summery outdoor plates on blue straw placemats with this blue vase of yellow daisies and tropical greenery. Fresh blueberries and linen napkins added more depth to this simple setting.

My Love of Palms

My friend Erika recently gave me these beautiful hand-painted plates. I could hardly wait to set this table with pink linen napkins in my palm-tree napkin rings, pink candleholders and silk peonies. The apple-green straw placemats added the just right pop of colour, and the pink water goblets echoed the pinks of the peonies and plate rims. Because it was brunch, instead of candles, I topped the palm tree holders with flowers.

Provence

For a brunch on the first day of spring, I placed my table, with its charming Provençal tablecloth, in front of the bright yellow forsythia bush. Black napkins provided a sophisticated contrast. The lemon centrepiece, the wicker water jug and bread completed this South of France–inspired table.

Sassy Flamingos

Ever since I saw the trained flamingos march in the Adastra Gardens in the Bahamas as a child, I've been in love with them. Would you believe everyone attending the Flamingo March was told to wear longer shorts, as the flamingos preferred that! On black straw placemats, I set fuchsia napkins in black napkin rings, white china, and the flamingo centrepiece.

Androsia and Starfish

Wrapped my Androsia batik fabric (from the island of Andros in the Bahamas) around the umbrella pole. I added two ceramic melon-coloured starfish to complement the melon napkins.

Beach House in Qualicum

While staying with my girlfriend Darla at her beach house at Qualicum on Vancouver Island, I surprised her with this setting: nautical-themed placemats and white napkins in red napkin rings, the driftwood, and a perfect seashell for my salt and pepper.

Table 1: Simple, with the tablecloth folded down the centre to make a runner. I let the fringe speak for itself!

Table 2: Changed the wine glasses and opened up the tablecloth slightly, anchoring it with the seashell and the large coral.

Moroccan Flair

Wandering through my house finding just the right treasures for each project is one of my favourite things to do. On location at Rothman & Co, which is unfortunately now closed, I saw these grey scalloped placemats; I knew this setting had to be Moroccan style. The smoky grey and gold votive candleholders were perfect with the dates in the small silver bowls. The orchid, native to Morocco, provided the height I wanted for this tabletop.

French Country

Decided to design a simple centrepiece here but using the same linens, china and stemware as in the Moroccan Flair. The silver doves, nesting on grey silk in the centre, a repurposed silk blouse of mine, and the assorted plants and hearts, provided the French countryside feel. All this table needed was a rough French loaf and some rosé to make it perfect.

Reading Room

I created a room in my home just for me, a special place to spend quiet mornings and afternoons. Spoil yourself sometimes. Find a quiet place in your home; a pretty mug or teacup and fresh flowers will soothe your spirit.

amore

Luncheons

This section includes a luncheon for one and a working lunch for two, as well as luncheons for larger groups, inside or outdoors. You can set a simple table or make a statement by dressing it up more formally.

Spring Has Sprung

With this table's cool colours, tone on tone, instead of using napkin rings, I tied the napkins and placed them on the flower plates. Because the matching runner was too bulky to lay flat, I wrapped it around the jug of fresh baby's breath with silk flowers on either side. No need for chargers this time, as the plates make their own statement. The clean lines and simplicity of this setting are classic.

Shades of Blue

I wanted this table to be laid back, relaxing. The placemats are two-toned, slightly faded. Loved using the blue plates with the smaller side plates from a different set, again in the blue tones. On top of the folded napkins, I added a white starfish. Centrepieces do not have to be a lot of work. In this case I happened to have the perfect faded candle holder and added silk florals on either side. Note that I feature cobalt blue water glasses and white to showcase two different looks.

Ladies' Luncheon by the Pool

This simple vase, with fresh and silk blooms, was a wedding gift to my parents many years ago. The lovely linen, silverware, crystal, green-leaf salad plates, turquoise fruit bowls and scattered silk petals mirror the gardens and swimming pool. Gilligan Girls Flowers on Main filled the vase so stylishly, mixing silk blooms with fresh blossoms and greenery.

Summer Stripes by the Sea

I had fun packing up the car and finding just the right picnic location by the sea. Using striped placemats and a simple straw runner, I added the large silver clamshell in the centre for cool drinks on ice. The centrepiece is a mix of nautical touches, netting and seashells. Had fun finding the fresh florals for napkin rings, and on the centrepiece I wrote the guests' names on white seashells.

Working Lunch

Even a lunch break in the office can be elegant. A soft grey Ralph Lauren tablecloth, matching napkins, silver votive candleholders and silk flowers finished this tablescape.

Understated Elegance

Silk blooms and silver bowls anchor this bold turquoise tablecloth. Matching napkins drape under the silver chargers with white candles at each end of the table.

Tumbling Seashells

My friend Susan called to say she discovered an unusual china seashell in her china cabinet and wondered if I would like to use it for a table setting. As soon as I saw it, ideas flowed for a shell-themed table for two. Using the china shell as a focus, with real seashells tumbling out onto the glass table, I added similarly themed napkins, rings, and side plates, with a real seashell at each place setting.

Red Poppies Delight

I wanted a bright yet simple tablescape. The white linen tablecloth was a good contrast with the square yellow placemats. The woven bread baskets from Merrimen's in Maui tie in with everything and keep the buns warm. The final touch was the silk poppies in a yellow china pot. The napkin rings tie in with the bread baskets and bamboo cutlery.

Birds of a Feather

Two exotic birds anchored the centre of this table for six. I added silk flowers from my collection of ribbons, ties and tassels, and wicker chargers on linen placemats. Yellow napkins in wooden napkin rings pick up the yellow in the mangoes and bananas in wicker containers and allowed the patina of the table to speak for itself.

Red Coral and Seashells on the Terrace

Fabulous rich corals were the inspiration for a table for four on the terrace. Coral placemats, napkins and runner completed this tropical setting. I also added tiny shells on each place card, along with grasses and scattered sand and seashells across the table. The coral rings around the pristine white napkins really stand out.

Flirty Flamingos

This flamingo runner cried out for flamingos all around: the lemonade carafe, salt and pepper shakers, napkins and cookies by Sugar Vancouver. The turquoise and hot pink accents and the green vase with its fresh pink gerberas added to the fun summer table. Notice the flamingo nesting on the water fountain.

All Aboard

My friend Joni lent me her father's 100-year-old red lantern, the focal point, with the large plastic anchor, of this nautical red, white and blue table. Salad plates in the same colours, red silk flowers, blue glass fisher's floats, the nautical scarf with its iron-on anchor and my father's vintage binoculars were unique touches.

She Sells Seashells

Fresh white antirrhinum topped a vase filled with seashells, surrounded with coral and more shells. Beneath this was a large sea-fan placemat. Fish-shaped plates atop folded napkins over white plates kept the outdoor glass table light and airy.

Dori

Luncheon by the Lake

I tailored this table overlooking Lake Okanagan, in the beautiful garden of my friends Liz and Jim. The focal point was the seagull perched atop the large glass container, with netting and shells both inside and around it. Turquoise beaded napkin rings, a nice contrast on the darker blue napkins, and silver chargers on the outdoor placemats were a classic touch. Olives in turquoise side dishes and citronella candles completed this summer table.

Family Barbecue

Everyone loves a barbecue. "Keep it simple and fun" is my motto. This red and white fabric, from Rokko Fabrics, was not quite long enough for the table, so I added a piece of red cloth down the middle. Plastic baskets with checkered paper liners were just right for hamburgers, hot dogs and chips. The watermelon in fancy shapes, pies from Krause Berry Farms, iced tea, cool and delicious with fresh lemon wedges, were a big hit. The borrowed popcorn machine, though, was the biggest hit of all!

Anchors Aweigh

The Royal Vancouver Yacht Club was the ideal place for this table for six. Starting with a wicker sailboat filled with assorted buns from the Valley Bakery in Vancouver, on a classic white tablecloth I arranged turquoise luncheon plates and white chargers on blue straw placemats. The blue napkin rings, with tiny turquoise and blue stones in the shape of anchors, were a lucky find and were stunning on the turquoise napkins. The cobalt blue water glasses and the small anchors and tiny sailboats sprinkled here and there completed the setting. Water and wine glasses filled, we sat down to shrimp starters while enjoying the view of the sailboats, ships and stunning North Shore mountains.

Hibiscus and Bougainvillea

These hibiscus plates on matching placemats are stunning! White plates provide just the right contrast. You could do this with solid pink or green plates as well. The silk bougainvillea in the smoky pink glass vase and scattered blooms on the table, along with the pink water goblets, completed this arrangement.

Apple of My Eye

The straw placemats, from my travels in Provence, on a white linen tablecloth made this a pared-down setting, simple but classic, with apples in a glass bowl in the centre. I made the napkin rings using artificial apple slices. Mints added a refreshing note. I made my mother's apple pie recipe and decorated it with food colouring to match the table decor.

Caribbean Influence

Sometimes less is more. The runner here certainly sets the mood for this bright tropical table. I decided to let it speak for itself, adding only red and white coral and turquoise glass chips on the table and in the red coral. Coral napkin rings and beach glass on the place cards carried the theme.

Ladies Who Lunch

I kept this small table simple, using leaf-patterned chargers with plain plates. I tied the cutlery with green twine and placed a fork under each napkin ring for the starter. Fresh greens in a potted china planter with gold cherubs anchored this table.

Erika

Mellow Yellow

A yellow straw purse designed by my talented friend Erika was the inspiration for this tabletop. Yellow cloth placemats with matching napkins echoed the yellow purse. I added the green lily plant to add some texture and to fill in the purse. The green candle holders blended beautifully with the glass green napkin rings. The final touch was a palm-tree plate. This is such a simple centrepiece, and you can have the handles up or down, cut some flowers from your garden, or pop in a plant as I did.

Artichokes, Anyone?

I set this table for two in front of a small loveseat, but it would be easy to add another chair. The artichokes in the centre and on each plate were all this table needed. Notice the runner on the round table, arranged in folds to fit the space — see the *Tips and Suggestions* section for more.

Lunch on a Bench

For small spaces, just pull up a table like this antique one in front of a bench or a window seat. With the orchid in the centre, a white linen placemat and a napkin ring dressed up with a silk orchid and greenery, you have an elegant setting for one. Kiwi on a fruit plate and a crystal goblet on the glass coaster complete this invitation to lunch.

Dinner Parties

When you're inviting family or friends over for dinner, it doesn't have to be formal. I tend to do easy and light meals outside in summer and go the more formal route in the winter. The memories you make and the laughter you share are the most important things . . . over a beautiful table, of course!

West Coast Vibes

The client's dining table in warm west-coast wood, with green ferns in a long white container, needed little more to set the tone here. Wooden beige, green and plum-coloured placemats, accompanied with green napkins in double napkin rings, enhanced the woodsy ambiance. I added twigs of heather under each napkin ring for added flair.

Fine Dining

It was an honour to create this table in one of Vancouver's premier stores for quality tableware and home decor, Atkinson's. Using their finest linen, exquisite china, silverware and crystal stemware, I created this stunning tabletop. Thomas Hobbs Florist designed the flower arrangement in the Baccarat Diva vase, which allows a horizontal arrangement. Love the whimsical crystal butterflies which added a bit of fun to this formal tabletop.

Boats and Bridges

I made the focal point of this table at Bridges, on Granville Island, the delightful seahorse centrepiece created again by Thomas Hobbs Florist. White table linen, blue napkins in beaded and silver rings, and a silver candle and chargers, with a scattering of blue stones, almost completed the setting. I draped the chairs with blue fabric, setting the stage for the fabulous view of passing sailboats and rowers.

All About Coral

My daughter Lani's coral tablecloth was the inspiration for this outdoor table setting. The napkin rings are two different styles but complement each other and the red coral in the tablecloth. I kept the table clean and simple with the long clear glass centrepiece holding rich corals and added white glass. I repeated the coral theme right down to seating cards with coral accents.

Festive Fruits and Veggies

This fall tabletop began with a floral runner, then added pomegranates, sugar apples, eggplants and artichokes, plus artificial greens and yellow florals. White and green china on gold chargers and glass votives provided a warm glow to the table.

Early Dinner by the Ocean

I so enjoy going to clients' homes or on location to set a tabletop, and this was a lovely day to set a table for an early dinner by the ocean. Once I covered the picnic table with my beautiful turquoise and white Androsia fabric (which you have seen wrapped around an umbrella pole in Androsia and Starfish in the Brunches section), and when the sunshine came out, I was ready to be creative. I added the straw fish-shaped placemats and placed the cutlery in the clear acrylic fish-shaped napkin rings with the turquoise linen napkins. In the centre of the table I placed a narrow platter fashioned as a salmon, seashells, netting and a piece of driftwood found on the beach, and glass balls continued the beach theme. Candles in Miraval rosé wine bottles filled with water waited to be lit when the sun went down.

Leaves Everywhere

Again, a basic setting: leafy placemats, wicker touches and bamboo cutlery. You could use matching napkins, white ones, or even coloured. As you can see, I decided to do two tables to showcase the way in which you could use the same placemats and napkins but with different centrepieces.

Table 1: For a casual luncheon or dinner for four, omit a runner or tablecloth. A centrepiece with green foliage and green candleholders with floating white candles sets a casual tone.

Table 2: Luncheon/dinner for eight. Use the same linens, glassware and cutlery as Table 1 but scatter green leaves on the mahogany table, add two tall hurricane shades with white candles, and centre a large white vase with green leaves.

Romance in the Air

I enjoyed creating this romantic table for two aboard a Spirit Cruises yacht in Vancouver Harbour. After champagne, the couple sat down on Chiavari chairs to a setting all in white and gold, with a stunning centrepiece by Suzanne of Granville Island Florist. I loved adding the gold sea-fans and brass candlesticks, which created magic after sundown. White linen with touches of gold in the napkin rings and chocolates in a Tiffany crystal box, and the scene was set!

Splendour in the Summer

I longed to use these beautiful but busy placemats that I've had for years. I knew the setting needed to be simple but elegant. With that in mind, I asked the talented Maureen, of Gilligan Flowers on Main, to create this beautiful fresh floral centrepiece. It tied in perfectly, not only with the table linens and placemats but with the room's decor as well.

Inspired by Citrus

Seeing lemon trees in Sorrento encouraged me to create this cheerful table, using lemons as an affordable and accessible centrepiece. This time I used both fresh and artificial lemons. The yellow pitcher and plate with banana bread picked up the yellow lemons in the placemats.

Crisp Green and White

I love using my Ralph Lauren runner and placemats; here I placed them on a white linen tablecloth and had matching white napkins with Martha Sturdy napkin rings, which you have seen in one of my New Year's tabletops. The runner was a bit long for my table of eight, so I twisted the ends, which added some style. I placed three glass containers with brass bottoms along the table and before filling them with water added a few opaque white and light green glass bits to give some depth. I decided to go with fresh blooms and greenery, placing fresh petals in the larger container but just floating candles in the smaller ones. The final touch to the centrepiece was two glass candle holders and green candles to give a bit of height. The Clarendon china, with gold cutlery and my best crystal, certainly dressed up this table. I have also styled this tabletop with white silk hydrangeas, which gives a simpler look, but I always add the fresh petals in whatever container I decide on.

White Linen and Orchids

A white linen tablecloth and white napkins established the all-white theme of this formal setting. Candles on a rustic silver mirror subtly lit the centrepiece. Silver accents in the charger plates, cutlery, lemon dish, wine decanter, and fluted goblets and butter dish added to its elegance.

Shades of White

For this formal wedding dinner I used the client's traditional china and crystal, on square beaded placemats with off-white lace-trimmed napkins in matching beaded napkin rings. I tucked a sprig of green with white beads into each napkin, scattering cream berries here and there. Port Moody Flowers designed three types of greenery for the centre of the table. I also decorated the mantel with a swathe of gold fabric and flowers, plus white candles in crystal candle holders in three hurricane lanterns.

Versailles

I created this grand table especially for you, my readers, at Fino Lino Fine Linens and Accessories. On this round table, I added this exquisite tablecloth and beautiful napkins. I loved mixing the silver and the greys on this table. The beautiful crystal wineglasses and silver accent balls blended so well with the decor. As I did here, you can have more than one set of candlesticks on a table, not necessarily identical or the same size. The elegant glass chargers were perfect, as you could see the fabric of the tablecloth. I so enjoyed the subtle stripes in the napkins, and the silver napkin rings were perfect and complemented the rest of the decor. The finishing touch was the fresh lavender from The Bloomerie Florist.

Black and White

There is nothing like dining outdoors in a quiet courtyard under the stars on a summer's evening. Black napkins on the black tablecloth, silk hydrangeas at the base of the candlesticks, a floating candle in a crystal bowl and white china. Champagne in crystal champagne flutes sets the mood for romance. Or perhaps intrigue?

Condo Dinner

This is an elegant presentation suitable for a table in limited space. White square plates on grey straw placemats, grey linen napkins in beaded crystal napkin rings, silver votive candle holders and silk flowers in the crystal and silver vase completed this setting. This same vase is a feature in my Working Lunch tabletop.

Greek Chic

I chose crisp white linens topped with an eye-catching indigo-ivy-motif runner, on to which I scattered fresh and silk fuchsia orchids. The blue and white china made quite a statement on its own. I wanted the centrepiece to add light and texture, which it certainly did, thanks to the very talented Jamey McDonald Designs, who blended fuchsia orchids with apple-green florals and shades of greenery. The clear chargers with beaded silver balls tied in beautifully with the sterling silver cutlery and the candle holders with hurricane lanterns.

Tortoiseshell and Tangerine

I delight in bright colours, often mixing them with interesting accessories to complement or contrast. Here, my inspiration was a tangerine scarf, paired with tortoiseshell votive candle holders, and used as a runner atop the black tablecloth. Simple black dishes on wooden chargers instead of placemats, a tortoiseshell bowl for bread sticks, an oblong bowl for tamarinds and dates, and tortoiseshell glasses added the finishing touches to this table.

Key Lime and Silver

These apple-green placemats appear in several of my tabletops in this book. I use them to brighten the table settings. I kept this tabletop very simple, with silver accents and a white linen tablecloth but different napkins, which were key lime with a pop of white. The silver votive holders tied in with the silver napkin rings and the centrepiece filled with green artichokes. For fun I sprinkled some silver stars and green berries around the silver container and added some greenery with berries around each wine stem. Quite often I mix linens and like the accents it gives.

Moira

Tahitian

I did not want to fuss too much with this tabletop. The wrought-iron table did not need dressing up with linen, but I could not resist these straw placemats, which make quite a statement on their own. I added three gold lanterns and some fresh green tropical leaves at either end. I placed the glass votive holders on the tan runner with gold and green accents. The gold cutlery worked well with the other gold touches in the runner and the lanterns.

Parrots and Tropical Leaves

My tablecloth with parrots and tropical foliage, actually a wall hanging, was ideal for this table for four. To highlight its beautiful fabric, I used clear charger plates. The centrepiece, greenery with kumquats, echoed the fabric's colours.

Al Fresco

A perfect summer evening inspired me to create a casual dinner for four on the patio. Starting with the sophisticated seashell runner, I added candles surrounded by seashells. I tucked the white napkins underneath the white dinner plates with small melamine plates decorated with seashells on top. (I mix and match china and melamine often — see *Tips and Suggestions*.) With my cozy seashell throw, a gift from my friend Tracy in Maui, casually draped over the sofa arm, we were ready for our night under the stars.

Get Togethers

This category, which falls in between lunches and dinners, is just a casual coffee or tea and sweets. We are always so busy these days, and it is important to stop every once in a while and smell the roses, or sit in the garden and enjoy your own company. Or you can have some guests in for a lovely cup of tea.

Purple Haze

This gorgeous tray, a gift from my cousin Wendy, is the focal point for the sweet pastries, fruit, purple napkin and coffee cup.

Coffee with a View

Mixing and matching for this coffee morning. Freshly picked flowers, linens and plates in soft greens, wicker chairs — all perfect for enjoying the Okanagan lakeside garden view.

Young Ladies at Tea

Wanting this to be delicate and airy, I set the table outside under a tree in full bloom. I rented the pink linen tablecloth, scattered it with crystals and petals from the tree and placed silk blossoms behind each chair. Pink tulle covered the missing handle of the silver teapot, a family heirloom. Port Moody Flowers designed the floral centrepiece. Each tea guest (children of dear friends) was given the china cup and saucer as a keepsake.

Tea Time

My friend Mina invited me over to set a tea table using her beautiful tea set with lovely bright colours. The gorgeous blue and gold tea set was complemented by the bright fuchsia silk flowers, and I added just one blue flower to tie in with the blue in the china. The simple fuchsia linen placemats with matching napkins were on white linen. I placed the flowers in a gold butter dish, as I wanted a bit of height.

Tea for Two

The same table as Young Ladies at Tea, set once again under the tree in bloom, now with my mother's teacups, blue and white with tiny pink blossoms. The delicate cutwork tablecloth with matching napkins came from the Bahamas thirty-five years ago.

Tea For Two

Sharks
in the runway
Sharks

Fall Picnic

What could be easier and more enjoyable than an autumn afternoon in Stanley Park! Pack your picnic basket with good French bread and cheese, pâté, some wine and apricots. Bring your favourite books or magazines and set everything out on a picnic blanket. Settle yourself to watch the boats go by on English Bay. Let the leaves fall as they may around you.

Happy Hour

I can well remember, growing up in the Bahamas, how special cocktail hour was for my beloved parents. My mother would change into a long cotton dress and my father into a smart shirt and slacks. This would take place in their beautiful living room overlooking the kidney-shaped pool and patio, or under large trees in the beautiful garden. I would sometimes surprise them with cocktail finger foods.

> "The pineapple is the symbol of social events, symbolizing welcome, friendship, and hospitality."
>
> Chef Blade

Cocktails at The Bar

My friend Roger gave me these smart black placemats with gold stars. I teamed them with gold napkins and black napkin rings. The gold-rimmed wineglasses were the perfect touch for this bar top setting.

Celebrations

I make a point of making each occasion feel special for my family and friends, whether we're celebrating someone's birthday, Easter, Thanksgiving, Christmas or New Year's Eve. I also create other opportunities to get together, like a good Oscar party! I hope you discover inspiration here for one of your tables!

Seashells and Flowers

I celebrated my daughter Shelley's fortieth birthday with this table in the garden. I built it around the silk floral and seashell centrepiece, coordinating it with multicoloured floral placemats and napkins. I repeated the seashell theme with the napkin rings. My friend Erika designed and painted the place cards, complete with tiny conch shells. And yes, there were edible seashells on the birthday cake.

Martin

Tropical Fruits and Exotic Florals

I celebrated my daughter Lani's fortieth birthday with Cuban flair: fans for the women and candy cigars for the men. Tropical fruits and exotic flowers in bright colours divided the table down the middle. Later, we served a special cake and coffee in another room lit with dozens of candles.

Pink and Blue

I wanted a pink and blue theme for the thirtieth birthday celebration of my twins, John and Jessica. I started with silk bougainvillea down the centre of the table and pink placemats cut to fit the large number needed for guests. Water glasses with turquoise swirls graced the table along with turquoise votive candleholders, turquoise napkins and simple napkin rings, to which I glued more bougainvillea blossoms. Finally, I made pink and blue place cards with the number thirty attached for each guest. As the sun went down and lights twinkled in the trees, candles flickered as we served individual birthday cakes to each twin.

X's and O's

A gold love sign, hearts, and pale pink linen placemats with pink plates topped with 'hugs and kisses' plates — what could be more romantic? The black and white striped ribbon was the perfect contrast.

Be Mine

My friend Iain brought me these Maxwell & Williams plates all the way from Sydney, Australia. Cindy of Party Tailor Balloons created the balloon garland, and Butter Baked Goods made the pastries. The deep-rose-coloured petals added a splash of colour to this all pink and white table.

Jessa

Love Is Red

The red tulips inspired me to do this simple Valentine's tabletop. I followed the red and white theme from the tulips to the red runner, on which I sprinkled petals and put floating candles in square containers with red petals. Notice the place cards were simple red hearts on which I wrote the guests' names in white.

The Shape of My Heart

Often something small inspires me, in this case, the mini hearts napkin rings. A pink scarf, with pink silk tulips in a pot, anchored the centrepiece. Valentine cookies placed on the heart-shaped plates were fun and delicious.

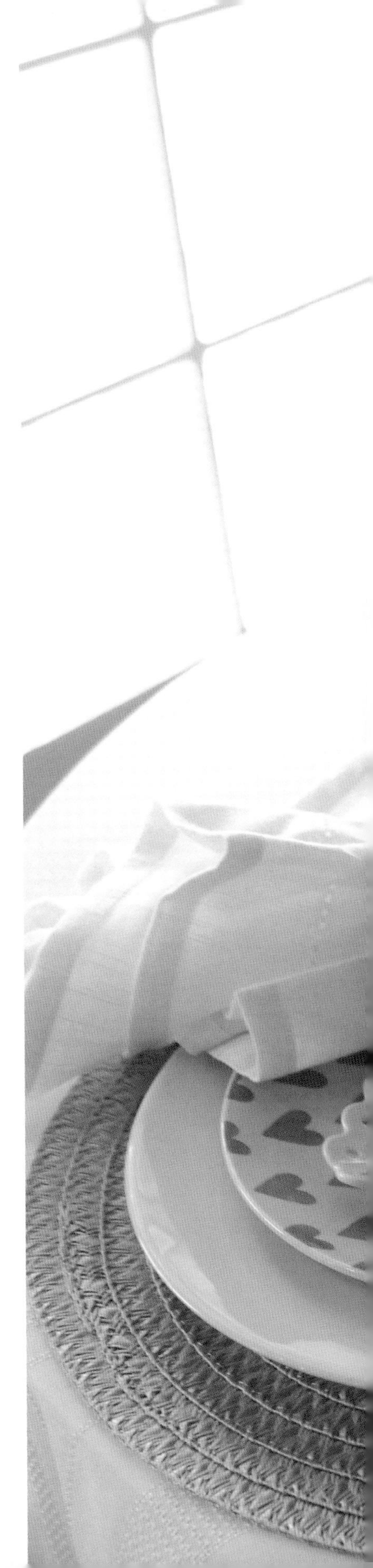

Pastels and Tulips

Starting with this delicate cutwork runner over a pale green tablecloth, I added china bunnies filled with candy Easter eggs and a vase of fresh tulips. At each place, I included, in silver napkin rings, white napkins with pink flowers, edged in green. Each guest's name was etched on a wooden bunny tied with a mint-green ribbon.

david

Martin

All About Bunnies

I used white hydrangeas between apple-green ceramics for this centrepiece. Using turquoise plates on silver chargers, I chose floral-patterned napkins to tie all the colours together. Silver bunnies held each guest's name. Making the Easter bunny cake with Smarties for ears was fun.

Yellows and Greens

This shows you how simple a table can be: white linens with a green runner down the centre of the table for six, simple folded napkins on top of each plate, and silver bunny card holders with each guest's name. Down the middle of the table are brass candlesticks with white candles, interspersed with white flowerpots filled with closed yellow tulips. Gold charger plates topped with white plates and scattered tulip petals complete this Easter tabletop.

Stripes and Ribbons

The brightly striped runner down the centre of this table, the turquoise linen tablecloth and the matching napkins incorporate all the Easter colours. I placed a large Easter basket in the middle, and I added yellow silk blooms and pink silk tulips, then tied yellow ribbons on either side of the basket. I used pastel tissue paper inside the basket, under a layer of coloured straw. I placed two Easter bunnies on top of the straw and surrounded them with assorted Easter eggs. The final touch was brightly coloured ribbons hanging from the crystal chandelier. For the place cards, I cut out bunnies in different colours and coordinated them with the coloured felt napkin rings. See *Tips and Suggestions* on how to make them. I loved the yellow silk flowers on either side of the basket, as well as the pink tulips, which all tied in with the ribbon I hung from the chandelier.

All About Pumpkins

Pale dried green leaves, and branches with white tiny buds, surrounded white pumpkins and white candles in gold candleholders down the centre of this table. The runner and placemats were white with pale green and beige leaves, with matching napkins. Each guest had a mini white pumpkin with their name written in gold, and went home with pumpkin cookies in a clear bag tied with orange ribbon.

thankful

Harvest Glory

I went hunting all over for the perfect real pumpkin to be the centerpiece of this tabletop. I carried the pumpkin theme throughout and added lots of fall colours and silks. Instead of candles I ran mini yellow lights throughout the foliage and pumpkins. Loved the individual pumpkin pies for each guest with their initials, which I special ordered from The Pie Hole. With such a large centerpiece I kept my linens simple, and dressed up my napkin rings with a 'thankful' tag and coloured the edges to make them pop. The mini pumpkins completed my overall theme.

Christmas Plaid

Using my plaid scarf, which matched the plaid placemats, I added candles, some gold glitter and a few tea lights. Ready for friends at lunch.

Martin

Santa Claus Is Coming to Town

It was a stroke of luck to find this beautiful old sleigh for my centrepiece. Lit with miniature lights and filled with Santa and his gifts, I set it in a bed of snow, adding pinecones and tiny Christmas decorations. White plates with green and gold rims sat on red chargers, topped with my hand-made crackers wrapped in foil and bearing miniature Santa name tags tied with red twine.

Christmas for Two

A red runner graced this beautiful mahogany table. In the centre, I filled a gold-rimmed crystal bowl with gold ornaments and glitter. Two gold Christmas trees, tied with sheer gold ribbon and with a few gold ornaments at their base, anchored this. Gold chargers and napkins in red napkin rings tied them all together like festive Christmas gifts.

Golden Hues

Golden hues describes the mood of this table, with its gold silk placemats and napkins in gold-beaded rings. Placing three different-sized battery-operated candles in gold candle holders on the wide satin runner, I added gold-edged leaves, gold pinecones, and gold Christmas ornaments. Tableware included my own Clarendon china, white with green and gold trim, on gold chargers, and gold-rimmed wineglasses. Guests found their way to their seats by looking for their names attached to fortune cookies on each side plate.

All That Glitters

I wanted this table to be sparkly and to display the Christmas trees of all shapes and sizes that I've collected for years. On the raw silk gold and silver fabric down the centre of the table, pearls and crystals glowed. I used white linen napkins with silver and gold accents under each plate. Silver chargers sat under white plates. My crackers are silver and white, with white Christmas trees edged in glitter tied with sheer silver ribbon. To make the table come alive, I used clear white glimmer strings. I also styled two accent tables using the same sheer silver ribbon as in the Christmas crackers, with gold and silver accents.

HAPPY
HAPPY

Starry New Year's Eve

Setting black placemats with gold stars on a black tablecloth was striking, and this time I doubled up on the napkins, which added contrast, as did the beaded gold napkin rings. The clear wineglasses had a sprinkling of gold stars which tied everything together beautifully. That only left the centrepiece, which I dressed in gold raw silk fabric, with white candles in elegant brass candlesticks. The final touches were the sprinkling of stars on the tablecloth and two gold-and-silver New Year's hats.

Hello, Gorgeous

The orchestra played "Some Enchanted Evening" when my mother and father met on New Year's Eve in the Bahamas. She wore a strapless black and gold cocktail dress, which I used as the fabric for this New Year's tabletop. 'Hello, Gorgeous' plates sat on gold chargers. I tied the gold and black napkins with my three-toned gold bracelet. We drank from the matching 'Hello, Gorgeous' wineglasses at midnight!

Hello,
orgeous

A Golden Touch

Wanting a clean but elegant table for this special evening, I began with a white linen tablecloth and added white plates on gold chargers, gold cutlery and gold raw silk napkins in Martha Sturdy napkin rings. For the centrepiece I separated a wreath piece by piece and added twinkling lights and some more fruit. Each guest had a single pear on their plate which had a tag reading 'Happy New Year!'

Happy New Year

NKELL

Snowy Day

On New Year's Day, we awoke to a snowfall. I used the basket on the garden bicycle to keep the beverages cool for our champagne and orange juice breakfast. A golden hat gave the final touch. Happy New Year!

Brea

Travelling Tables

I love travelling and experiencing the culture and people of the country I am visiting. I am always on the lookout to set a table under an old tree by the ocean, or in a quaint and charming restaurant, a wine bar, or a café. Naturally, when travelling you are discovering new tastes and foods, and I thought I would share some of my favourite recipes with you from dear friends, chefs and restaurants. Enjoy!

Renaissance

When visiting the ancient and historic city of Florence, one of our favourite places in Italy, my husband and I stayed in a stunning apartment right in the middle of the city. It was as if we were staying in someone's private home. Stepping back in time, as I walked through the beautifully decorated rooms, I collected pieces to grace our Renaissance table: a tassel on an antique desk, a plump cherub, a curtain tieback. Finally, I added my own gold chain.

Pici or Bucatini with Pancetta

INGREDIENTS (SERVES 2–3)

- 2 medium white onions
- 1 tbsp extra virgin olive oil
- 200 grams of pasta such as pici* or bucatini
- 80 grams of cubed pancetta or a thick bacon
- ½ cup of a full-bodied red wine
- 1 bottle (680 ml) of *passata* (strained tomatoes)
- ½ tsp fresh thyme, chopped fine
- ¼ tsp salt and ¼ tsp freshly ground pepper (to taste)
- Parmesan cheese

* *Pici* is a thick spaghetti-type pasta found in Tuscany. *Bucatini* pasta is easier to find in Italian food stores.

PREPARATION

1. Chop the onions.
2. In a heavy frying pan on medium low, add the olive oil.
3. Add onions and slowly cook until soft and translucent. Stir to ensure they are not browning.
4. Add the cubed pancetta and the red wine and cook until the wine evaporates.
5. Add the *passata* and one cup of warm water.
6. Add in the thyme, salt and the pepper. Put a lid partially on the pot and simmer for approximately 45–50 minutes. Taste halfway through and if necessary add more thyme, salt or pepper.
7. Prepare a large pot of boiling water. Generously add salt to the boiling water. Add the pasta and stir occasionally. Boil the pasta for 1 minute less than the instructions on the box. It should be al dente. Do not drain the pasta.
8. Slowly lift the pasta out of the water with tongs and add to the simmered sauce in the fry pan. Toss until coated. Add some of the pasta water, if needed, to fortify the sauce.
9. Place in a serving bowl and grate some Parmesan cheese to your liking over the top. You can include a small bowl of grated Parmesan if people would like more.
10. Serves 2 people for dinner or 3 if a side for lunch.

RECIPE BY FOLCO GAMBERUCCI

Stuffed Zucchini

INGREDIENTS (SERVES 6)

- 6 medium zucchinis, left whole
- 2 tbsp extra virgin olive oil
- ½ red onion, finely chopped
- 6 cloves garlic, minced
- Salt
- Freshly ground black pepper
- Dash of cayenne pepper
- 3 large eggs
- ½ cup freshly grated Parmesan cheese
- ½ tsp grated nutmeg
- 2 tbsp chopped fresh parsley

PREPARATION

1. Preheat the oven to 350°F.
2. Blanch the zucchinis for approximately 6 minutes in a large pot of boiling water, then remove from the water and cut in half lengthwise.
3. Scoop out the middle of each zucchini, creating a trough in the centre.
4. Leave enough pulp around the edges so the zucchinis won't collapse as they cook.
5. In a sauté pan heat the olive oil and add the onion, garlic and scooped-out zucchini centres, as well as salt, pepper and cayenne to taste. Cook for approximately 4 to 5 minutes, or until the mixture is cooked and soft.
6. Remove the mixture from the sauté pan and put into a food processor. Add the eggs, parmesan, nutmeg and parsley to the food processor as well and process to a moist consistency and a mousse-like texture.
7. Fill each hollowed-out zucchini with the processed mixture and place in a baking dish. Bake in oven for 20–30 minutes.
8. Serves 6 as a main course, 12 as a side vegetable.

Tiramisu

INGREDIENTS (SERVES 6)

- 3 large eggs
- 3 tbsp sugar
- ¼ cup mascarpone cheese
- ⅓ cup fresh espresso, cooled
- ¼ cup cognac
- 1 large package ladyfingers (5 oz)
- Cocoa powder for dusting

PREPARATION

1. Separate the eggs into two medium bowls. With an electric mixer, beat the whites with the sugar until stiff peaks form.
2. In the other bowl, use the mixer to cream the yolks and mascarpone to a smooth consistency. Gently fold the cheese mixture into the whites.
3. Stir the espresso and the cognac together in a flat-bottomed dish and dip the ladyfingers quickly into the liquid, one at a time. The secret is to allow them to absorb a bit of the liquid but not so much that they fall apart.
4. Place one-third of the dipped ladyfingers in an 8-inch (2 L) square glass baking dish. Spread one-third of the mascarpone mixture over the ladyfingers. Repeat with each of the next third of ladyfingers, ending with the mascarpone mixture.
5. Dust the top with cocoa powder.
6. Refrigerate for at least 2 hours before serving.
7. Tiramisu is best served the next day. It can also be frozen and then thawed for a couple of hours before serving.

RECIPE BY UMBERTO MENGHI

Santorini Blue

A family luncheon for four in a stunning villa overlooking the ocean. I so enjoyed hunting through the bright kitchen for all the pieces to create this simple but pretty tabletop. The centrepiece was flowers and greenery from the surrounding garden. With such a view I kept it clean and simple, using what I could find: colourful plates, the tablecloth and other bits and pieces.

Roast Leg of Lamb

RECIPE BY MARYANN NEZIS

INGREDIENTS (SERVES 6–8)

- 5–6 lb leg of lamb
- 3 garlic cloves, slivered
- ½ cup lemon juice
- 1 tbsp oregano
- Salt and pepper to taste
- Water

PREPARATION

1. Remove all visible fat from lamb, wash and dry. Make slits in lamb and insert garlic slivers.
2. Place lamb in baking pan and sprinkle with lemon juice. Rub with oregano and season with salt and pepper.
3. Cover pan and marinate in refrigerator for several hours.
4. To roast the lamb, add a cup of water to the pan for basting. You may have to add more as it cooks. Roast the lamb, uncovered, at 350°F for 1½ hours for pink and 2 hours for well-done.
5. Serve with orzo, rice or roasted potatoes. Add any of these ingredients half an hour before lamb is cooked.

Semolina Cake (Ravani)

INGREDIENTS (SERVES 8–10)

- 12 large eggs, separated
- ¾ lb unsalted butter
- 1 cup sugar
- 1 cup farina or semolina
- 1 cup flour
- 4 tsp baking powder

SYRUP INGREDIENTS

- 4 cups sugar
- 3 cups water
- 1 tsp lemon juice

PREPARATION

1. Grease an 8" by 12" pan.
2. Combine dry ingredients.
3. Beat butter and sugar well with electric mixer.
4. Add egg yolks one at a time and beat well.
5. Combine with dry ingredients.
6. Beat egg whites until soft peaks form, and fold into the batter.
7. Bake at 350°F for about 40 minutes, or until the cake is golden and shrinks lightly from the sides of the pan.
8. Prick the surface with a fine skewer or toothpick to test if done.
9. Boil syrup for ½ hour and then pour over cake.

RECIPE BY EVANGELIA KASDTRENAKES

Bread

Good Morning

While sailing on a private Turkish gulet, I offered to create a breakfast tablescape. The captain said, "Of course, Madam!" and off I went. I found some seashells and wrapped a bracelet of mine around a condiment jar. After sitting down to enjoy the breakfast of fresh buns, fruit, cheeses, meats, olives and tomatoes, we were greeted by a smiling fisherman who yelled "Good morning!" as he motored by. The chef was fishing off the side of our yacht and the crew was polishing the rich mahogany. Indeed, it was a moment to treasure.

Shrimp and Vegetable Clay Pot Casserole (Karides Güveç)

INGREDIENTS (SERVES 6–8)

- 1 lb fresh or frozen shrimp
- 1 medium onion, diced
- 2–3 cloves garlic, diced
- 3 tbsp olive oil
- 2–3 Hungarian wax peppers, or 1–2 green bell peppers
- 3 medium ripe tomatoes
- 1 cup fresh or canned small button mushrooms
- 1 tbsp tomato paste
- 1 tsp salt
- ¼ tsp black pepper
- ¼ tsp hot red pepper flakes (optional)
- 1 cup grated fresh Turkish *kashar* cheese, or other mild yellow cheese

PREPARATION

1. Fill a medium saucepan with water and bring to a boil. Add about 1 teaspoon of salt. Add the frozen or fresh shrimp. Boil for 1 to 2 minutes only. Drain the shrimp and run them under cold water to prevent further cooking.
2. Peel and dice the onion, garlic cloves and tomatoes. Clean the green peppers and dice them about the same size as the tomatoes. Drain or clean the mushrooms.
3. Heat the olive oil in a saucepan and fry the onions and garlic until they soften and become transparent. Add the green peppers and cook a few minutes more. Add the diced tomato, mushrooms, tomato paste, and spices and let the mixture simmer until most of the liquid is gone.
4. Add the cooked shrimp and gently turn the mixture with a wooden spoon to evenly distribute the shrimp throughout. Transfer the mixture into one large or several small clay pots or ovenproof dishes. Cover the top(s) generously with grated cheese.

RECIPE BY NEYZEN TRAVEL AND YACHTING

Baked Eggplant (Karnıyarık)

INGREDIENTS (SERVES 4)

- 3 lb Japanese eggplant or other oblong eggplant
- 2 cups vegetable oil for frying
- 4 tbsp olive oil
- 3 medium onions
- 7 ripe medium tomatoes
- 3 medium green or red bell peppers
- 1.5 lb ground beef
- 3 tbsp tomato paste
- 2 cloves garlic, finely chopped
- 2 tsp salt
- ½ tsp black pepper
- ½ tsp red pepper flakes
- 1 cup chopped Italian parsley leaves

PREPARATION

To prepare the eggplant:

1. Using a vegetable peeler or sharp knife, peel alternate strips from the eggplant end to end, leaving a striped pattern. Let the eggplants soak in heavily salted water while you prepare the other ingredients.

To prepare the filling:

1. In a large skillet, fry the onions in olive oil until tender and reduced. Add the ground beef and brown thoroughly.
2. Using a sharp paring knife, peel 5 of the tomatoes and dice them. Once the meat is nicely browned, add the tomatoes and continue stirring. You can also substitute canned diced tomatoes for fresh. Drain off the juice before adding them to the meat.
3. Add spices and garlic and stir well. Add the chopped parsley. Stir the mixture about 3 minutes more, then turn off the heat and let it rest.
4. Drain the eggplants and blot them dry with paper towels. In another skillet, heat the vegetable oil and fry the eggplants whole, turning them to cook evenly on all sides. When the eggplants soften, remove them from the oil and drain them on paper towels.
5. Line up the fried eggplants side by side in an ovenproof baking dish. Using your paring knife, cut a slit from end to end of each eggplant and gently open each with your fingers.
6. Fill the centre of each eggplant with the meat mixture. Slice the two extra tomatoes thinly, cut each slice in half, and place the slices over the filling. Do the same with the peppers.
7. Mix the water with the tomato paste and pour it into the baking dish. Cook the eggplant in a 375°F oven for about 30 minutes. Remove the dish from the oven and let it rest for a few minutes before serving.

RECIPE BY NEYZEN TRAVEL AND YACHTING

Marie

Modern Elegance

I embraced the opportunity to create a tabletop at a modern art-filled home in Beverly Hills. The dining room dictated understated elegance, so I styled this square glass table with simple placemats dressed up with sheer napkins in plain napkin rings. I filled the exquisite Lalique vase with tall white chrysanthemums, adding a Lalique lion and a smaller Lalique vase. The place cards were simple, with gold trim in glass holders, and I sprinkled glass stones here and there on the beautiful glass tabletop. My assignment here was to provide a setting for the paintings, which were for sale and which, indeed, did sell within a few days for a very large amount.

McCarthy Salad

RECIPE BY THE BEVERLY HILLS HOTELS & BUNGALOWS

INGREDIENTS (SERVES 4)

- ¼ head iceberg lettuce
- ½ head romaine lettuce
- ½ cup diced, grilled free-range chicken
- ½ cup diced, roasted red beets
- ¼ cup free-range egg yolk
- ¼ cup free-range egg white
- ½ cup finely diced aged cheddar cheese
- ½ cup applewood-smoked bacon
- ¼ cup diced tomato
- ¼ cup diced avocado

FOR THE DRESSING

- 1 cup Sparrow Lane balsamic vinegar
- 1 shallot
- 1 tbsp brown sugar
- 3 cloves roasted garlic
- 1 tsp Dijon mustard
- Kosher salt and black pepper to season
- Canola oil

PREPARATION

1. Arrange the salad ingredients in a bowl.
2. Place all the dressing ingredients in a blender and drizzle in canola oil to emulsify.
3. Mix the salad and dressing together, adjusting ingredients to your personal preference.

The Beverly Hills Hotel's most famous salad has been a favourite ever since regular guest and captain of the local polo team Neil McCarthy requested it in 1948.

Bahamian Rhapsody

When planning a tablescape, I often start with the centrepiece, in this case, my purple sea-fan, now sprayed white, two white corals, a candle and more seashells on a bed of sand. Here, the sand is from the island of Abaco in the Bahamas and Love Beach in Nassau. The coral placemats, picking up the colours of the plates, were a nice contrast to the white tablecloth and the runner. Napkins were tan to match the runner down the centre. At the last minute, I chose to mix and match the china by adding small side plates in two colours which tied in beautifully with the sea life pattern. Loved adding the seashells and other wee touches to make up this centrepiece, so reminiscent of the Bahamas, where I grew up and lived for many years before moving to Vancouver.

Johnny Cake

INGREDIENTS (SERVES 8–10)

- 5 cups flour
- ½ cup butter, room temperature to fold into pastry
- 1 cup sugar; reserve 2 tsp for dusting cake after baking
- ½ cup water
- ½ tsp salt
- 2 tsp baking powder
- ¾ cup of milk
- 1 egg yolk and 1 tbsp butter (whipped)

PREPARATION

1. Preheat oven to 325°F.
2. With mixer, or by hand, in large bowl mix flour, butter and sugar until thick but well blended.
3. Add water, salt and baking powder; mix together.
4. Slowly add milk.
5. Add egg yolk and whipped butter and mix. (Dough will be firm and slightly sticky to fingers.)
6. Remove from bowl and let rest on floured surface for about 20 minutes.
7. Place dough in a greased 10" by 10" pan. Let rest for 10 minutes.
8. Bake on centre oven rack.
9. Check after 45 minutes (colour should be light brown and centre should be slightly raised).
10. If not ready after 45 minutes, check every 5 minutes.
11. Once Johnny cake is baked, brush lightly with whipped egg yolk mixture and dust with reserved sugar. Let rest until cool enough to eat.

RECIPE BY THE POOP DECK SANDY PORT

Boiled Fish

INGREDIENTS (SERVES 6)

- 2 lb fresh Nassau grouper or other white fish
- Grouper bones or head chopped into pieces
- 2 medium white potatoes
- 2 medium white onions
- Sea salt to taste
- Hot pepper to taste
- 8 cups water per serving
- 6 medium limes per serving
- Vegetable oil

PREPARATION

1. Clean grouper.
2. Season grouper with sea salt, fresh lime juice and hot pepper to taste (best to keep fish on the bone).
3. Portion grouper for serving, (½ lb serves two).
4. Peel and dice onions.
5. Peel and cut potato into bite-size chunks.
6. Once grouper is marinated (minimum 30 minutes), coat bottom of medium stock pot with vegetable oil (only coat bottom, discard excess oil if necessary) and heat over medium heat.
7. Add potatoes to pot, stirring to avoid any burning. Repeat until exterior is sealed. Add part of the sea salt.
8. Add onions, continuing to stir, then add half a cup of water to pot, stir, and let sit until potatoes are almost cooked.
9. Add the bones of the grouper or pieces of the fish head to the water and continue cooking. Place cover on pot to bring to a boil.
10. Remove cover, turn down flame, add remaining water, stir, place fish on top of potatoes, bones and onions. Add additional lime and hot pepper, bring back to a boil, turn off flame. Keep pot covered for 10 to 15 minutes to allow dish to settle.
11. With large spoon, remove fish and place in bowl. Add the cooked potatoes and onions. Add additional hot pepper and lime to taste.

RECIPE BY THE POOP DECK SANDY PORT

Conch Fritters and Calypso Sauce

RECIPE BY COMPASS POINT RESTAURANT

INGREDIENTS (SERVES 6)

- 1 lb tenderized cut conch
  (you can substitute lobster or crab)
- 1 tbsp baking powder
- 2 tbsp tomato paste
- ¼ green bell pepper, finely chopped
- ¼ red bell pepper, finely chopped
- ¼ large onion, finely chopped
- ¾–1 cup water (depending on humidity)
- 2 cups all-purpose flour
- 1 tsp thyme, finely chopped

PREPARATION

1. Mix everything in a large bowl, and let rest for 15 minutes.
2. Pinch 1 tbsp of mixture and deep fry in oil, flipping when brown on one side.
3. Use a toothpick to determine when centre is cooked, and serve hot with calypso sauce.

To prepare the calypso sauce:

1. Mix equal parts mayonnaise and ketchup with a few dashes of hot sauce and a squeeze of fresh lime juice.

Fried Plantain

INGREDIENTS (SERVES 8–10)

- 5 or 6 ripe plantains
- 3 tbsp brown sugar
- Cooking oil

RECIPE BY SUSAN HYATT

PREPARATION

1. Peel the plantains
2. Cut in half and then again
3. Put oil on pan so it fully covers the plantain
4. Heat oil until it is sizzling
5. Arrange plantains so they're not on top of each other
6. Deep fry plantains until golden
7. Turn around and leave until golden
8. Remove with a slotted spoon and let oil drip
9. Spread some paper towel and put them on top
10. Let towel absorb all the excess oil
11. Put on plate and serve
12. If you want, you can sprinkle some brown sugar on top

Tropical Vibrations

As soon as I saw the wicker chest in our condominium in Maui, I knew it would be perfect for my Maui tabletop. I woke up early and went barefoot around the beautiful grounds collecting hibiscus blossoms and colourful croton and palm leaves. Starting with two fish napkin rings, I chose turquoise straw placemats with orange napkins and top plates that blended with the orange in the napkin rings. Here again, I improvised, using one of my scarves as an accent.

Fish Cakes with Tropical Salsa

INGREDIENTS (SERVES 6)

- 1 lb assorted fish, finely chopped
- ¼ cup scallions, finely chopped
- ¼ cup red bell pepper, finely chopped
- 1 garlic clove, finely chopped
- ½ cup mayonnaise
- 2 eggs, slightly beaten
- Salt and pepper to taste
- 2 cups panko flakes
- ½ cup peanut oil

TROPICAL SALSA INGREDIENTS

- 1 cup diced papaya
- ½ cup diced mango
- ½ cup diced red bell pepper
- 1 tbsp minced fresh jalapeño chili
- 1 tbsp chopped fresh cilantro
- 2 tbsp lime juice
- Salt

PREPARATION

1. Combine fish, scallions, peppers, garlic, mayonnaise and eggs, blending well.
2. Form into cakes.
3. Coat with panko flakes.
4. Refrigerate to chill.
5. Heat oil in skillet and add fish cakes.
6. Sauté cakes in peanut oil until browned on both sides.
7. Serve with tropical salsa.

To prepare the tropical salsa:
1. In a bowl, mix all the ingredients and add salt to taste.

RECIPE BY TRACY FLANAGAN

Banana, Lemongrass and Coconut Soup

INGREDIENTS (SERVES 8–10)

- ¼ cup olive oil
- 1 cup very ripe sliced bananas
- 1⅓ cups chopped onion
- 1 cup chopped leeks (white and pale green parts only; about 2)
- 1 cup chopped celery
- ¾ cup chopped carrots
- 3 garlic cloves, chopped
- 1 tbsp minced lemongrass (from bottom 2 inches; tough outer stalks removed)
- ½ tsp hot chili paste
- ¼ cup chopped fresh cilantro
- 1 tsp ground cumin
- 1 cup fresh orange juice
- 2 14-oz cans vegetable broth
- 1 14-oz can unsweetened coconut milk

PREPARATION

1. Heat oil in heavy large saucepan over medium-high heat.
2. Add bananas; sauté until beginning to brown, about 4 minutes.
3. Add onion, leeks, celery, carrots, garlic, lemongrass, chili paste.
4. Sauté until vegetables begin to brown, about 10 minutes.
5. Add cilantro and cumin.
6. Reduce heat to medium and sauté 2 minutes.
7. Add orange juice; simmer 2 minutes.
8. Add broth and simmer until vegetables are tender, about 10 minutes.
9. Cool soup slightly.
10. Working in batches, puree soup in blender until smooth. Return soup to pan.
11. Add coconut milk and warm, about 5 minutes.
12. Season to taste with salt and pepper.

RECIPE BY TRACY FLANAGAN

Mistral III

Tips and Suggestions

I believe it's important that you enjoy setting your table and have fun rather than seeing it as a chore. Having grown up in the Bahamas, I love outside entertaining. Yes, even in Vancouver, where it tends to rain a lot!

Building Your Tabletop

Decide ahead of time what type of mood you want to create. Will it be casual, elegant or grand? Will it be inside or outside?

For those of you who don't have an outside area, you can bring the outside in with your various tabletops, as you see in the tables that I showcase throughout this book. Do you need to purchase any items before setting your table, or do you have them on hand?

TIP: If you have eight guests and only six matching placemats, just add two different placemats at the ends of the table — but try to make them blend by using the same colour shades.

Decide what you will be using: a tablecloth, placemats or both? Runner down the centre? What about plate chargers? Once you have decided on inside or out and the type of table you would like to do, the fun begins.

I develop a vision before I set a table: the lighting, linens, centrepiece, plates, cutlery, glassware, colours — although not necessarily in that order. The most important thing to remember about tabletops and entertaining is to create an atmosphere where your guests feel relaxed and can have fun.

LIGHTING

There is nothing like a burning candle, but be careful. I use only battery candles on my formal dining room table, but occasionally I use real ones outdoors.

TIP: When you have burned your candle right down and are left with just the glass container, soak it and use it again for mini floral arrangements with water, or place a battery votive in it for the table or guest bathroom.

There are also battery lights you can set in water to light up a floral arrangement, or the bases that light up a crystal bowl. I tend to use a lot of the battery-operated string lights, as in my Happy New Year table centrepiece and others.

CANDLES, LANTERNS, VOTIVES OR MINI LIGHTS

When setting your table outdoors, please do not place your candles outside in sunlight too soon. Wait until the sun is gentler, towards the end of the day, or the candles will bend and melt.

I love lanterns on and off the table and mix different shapes, sizes, heights and colours. Gone are the days when you had only candles. Sometimes I do a combination of candles (battery usually), lanterns and votives.

I quite often use floating candles in a bowl with petals, or mini lights or glimmer strings, which come in all colours and are fun to use on tables also.

Outdoor lighting is magical and sets the mood for any occasion.

CENTREPIECES

I usually think of my centrepieces a few days ahead, and if I need to purchase something extra, I can do so then. To me, the centrepiece is the 'life' of the table! Have fun with your centrepieces! You can use fresh flowers from the garden or flowers from a florist. I love mixing fresh blooms with silk — see my paragraph on florals.

I also like using things like real rope, in all sizes, and netting when doing a nautical tabletop. In the Birds of a Feather tabletop I use green seam-binding, which added texture to the centrepiece.

Fresh and artificial fruits are also wonderful in centrepieces. Veggies (real and artificial) appear on my tabletops, like a bowl of tomatoes, or fruit, like mandarin oranges.

You do not always have to use florals in your centrepieces. In my Sassy Flamingos brunch tabletop, a ceramic flamingo on its own makes quite a statement. Speaking of flamingos, in my Flirty Flamingos tabletop the runner is the main focus. In my Tumbling Seashell tabletop, it is the ceramic seashell. In the Birds of a Feather tabletop, hands down it was the exquisite birds that anchored this table.

In the Anchors Aweigh tabletop, the natural sea-to-sky view is fabulous, but the sailboat in the centre filled with assorted buns is eye-catching. Looking at the Family Barbecue tabletop, it's the red and white tablecloth that draws you in.

FLORALS

I mix fresh blooms with silk flowers on my tables, as seen in the Luncheon by the Pool floral centrepiece. Here I blend silk florals with fresh greenery. Quite often I use all silks, which are increasingly natural-looking.

Or you can splurge a little and place an order with one of your favourite florists to fill a vase or provide you with fresh greens. I did this in the Shades of White tabletop, where I have three types of fresh greenery right down the centre. I also did it in Tahitian, where I have a mixture of tropical greenery down the centre with white orchids. Picking greenery or flowers from your garden is always lovely.

NAPKINS

When purchasing linen or cloth napkins, I find I get more use out of plain ones that I can reuse with different settings; the patterned ones don't give you as much flexibility. In my Flirty Flamingos tabletop, I show you how lovely a beautiful paper napkin can look, compared to the linen ones I'm using in Sassy Flamingos. I am always on the lookout for pretty paper napkins for future tables.

The linen napkins take more care and ironing, whereas if you get a blend of fabric, you can throw the napkins in the dryer and onto the table.

You can do all types of folds for napkins, or even tie them in the middle. Napkins can be folded and placed on a plate or folded long and placed under a plate — you have seen numerous examples of both methods throughout these pages.

TIP: Never iron a tablecloth on your table, even if you have a table pad on first. You will notice light white marks on your table. To my horror, this happened to me. I always put up my ironing board now. To get white heat marks off your table, place a white dishcloth over the mark. Turn on your iron and set to steam, then just gently tap over the spot using steam and it should be gone.

LINENS

Set your table protectors on first if you're setting a table that you need to protect. Then place your tablecloth or placemats, fabric or hard backed — see West Coast Vibes, where I used hard placemats. A tablecloth, as opposed to placemats, immediately sets the tone for a more formal setting, whether you're entertaining inside or outside.

RUNNERS

If you decide to use a runner to add more depth to your table, you can use one featuring a pattern or design, or a plain one. If you're using a very detailed runner, you can go with simple placemats or linen. Note how in my Caribbean Influence tabletop I had a very elaborate beaded runner, so the entire table revolved around it. I love runners and sometimes will just use a runner instead of placemats when I'm hosting a friend for lunch.

DIFFERENT WAYS TO USE RUNNERS

A runner does not hang well on a round table, so what I do is fold it on each end or in the middle. If you're using placemats and have a matching runner, it sometimes is too busy and too tight to use the runner in the traditional way, down the centre. If you have a larger table, by all means use both. I have sometimes folded the runner when using matching placemats. There is always a way. You can twist the runner on the ends or fold or scrunch it up at the ends and in the middle — see my All that Glitters Christmas tabletop.

PLATES

Again, like the napkins, I prefer the plain colours, as you can use them over and over again with different settings. If I use plates with a pattern, I use plain napkins.

Mix and match. You can use a plate with a pattern and then put a solid-coloured smaller plate on top, or vice versa. I mix and match my sets for casual entertaining and go more traditional in my dining room.

CHARGERS

If you decide to use chargers, you'll find them very versatile. I like the wooden ones I used in my Tangerine and Tortoiseshell tabletop. The rattan chargers used in my Birds of a Feather tabletop are lovely as well, for inside or outside.

I tend to use chargers instead of placemats when I am entertaining eight or more, as they allow more space around the table. Glass chargers will show off a lovely tablecloth underneath, as in my Parrots and Tropical Leaves tabletop, or you can place a single bloom or leaf under the charger. You can purchase chargers in all colours and finishes.

FINE CHINA VERSUS EVERYDAY

Do not keep your fine china in cabinets. Use it and enjoy. I love using my own Clarendon fine china, and my mother's Royal Worcester as well. In almost forty years of entertaining, I have yet to break a single piece of my Clarendon china. However, I am finding that most couples now use the everyday dishwasher-safe plates.

Going with classic white is a good buy, as it is so versatile and a blank canvas. You can add colour or patterns on top of a white dinner plate. I also mix melamine plates over fine china plates — see my Hibiscus and Bougainvillea tabletop.

CUTLERY

Sterling or good silver cutlery is lovely when setting a formal tabletop. I use my bamboo cutlery outdoors all the time, as well as my everyday cutlery with white handles, or everyday stainless steel. I use gold cutlery for formal tabletops.

CRYSTAL AND GLASSWARE

I always make sure my centrepiece is in place before setting my glassware. I still use my wedding crystal, which is priceless but beautiful. If you have fine crystal, use it. But of course not everyone has extensive glassware. You can mix and match with whatever you have available. Just have fun doing it!

NAPKIN RINGS

I have been collecting these for years. If you don't have enough of the same napkin rings for a larger table, I suggest using ribbon, twine or coloured rope. I sometimes use felt napkin rings in contrasting colours, like in my Easter Stripes and Ribbons tabletop.

Growing up in the Bahamas, we used cloth napkins daily, which were laundered when needed. My sister Andrea and I had our initials on our silver napkin rings.

TIP: I never put fine china, crystal or sterling silver in the dishwasher.

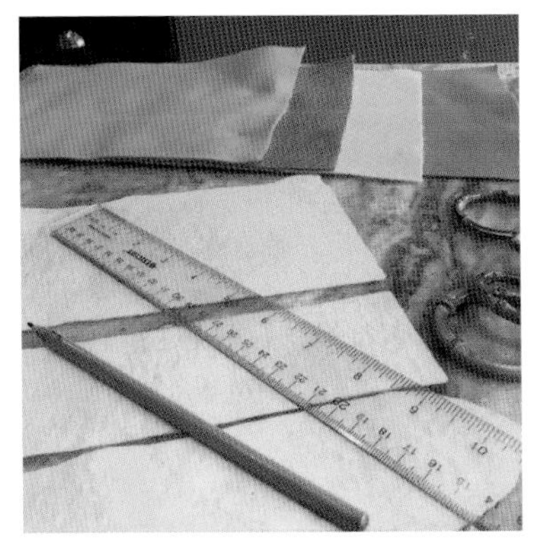

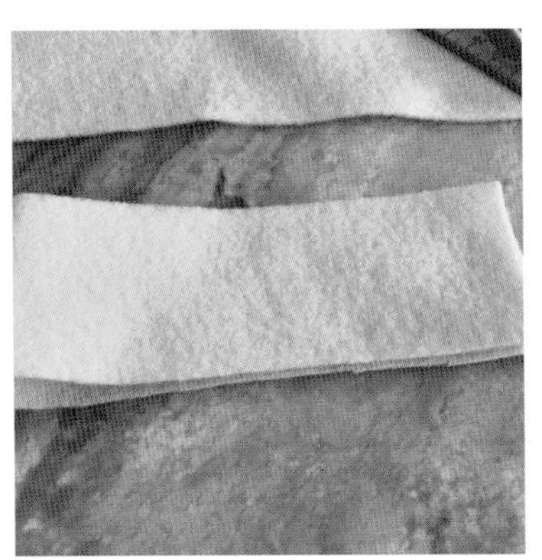

PLACE CARDS

I often design and make my own or add a line of colour around the edges of commercial ones. Place cards are optional but a nice personal touch that can also be helpful when hosting more than six guests.

LOCATION, LOCATION, LOCATION

Where do you set a table? Do it anywhere. Entertain in various rooms, inside or outside your house, townhouse or condo. I sometimes entertain in my family room, where I have a table, or at my bar that seats six. I tend to use the dining room for more formal gatherings — luncheons or dinners.

I even set tables in my home office if I am doing a working lunch, and have pulled my antique coffee table over to my window bench in my formal living room. I have set tabletops on kitchen islands or on tables in the kitchen. If you have a garden, what could be lovelier than some Chinese lanterns and lights in the trees and a beautiful table?

CONDO OR SMALL-SPACE LIVING

Sometimes, for a change, book the inside or outdoor rooftop area if it's available. Many condos have lovely party rooms. You can have guests over and serve drinks in your condo or apartment and then move them to the party room for dinner. I have served dinner on my upper courtyard and afterwards had the guests come down to the lower courtyard, where I served coffee and desserts. TV tables come in handy on a narrow sundeck, and you can dress them up with placemats and a small votive candle.

THEME TABLES

When entertaining, you can transport your guests to faraway places like Hawaii, Mexico and the Caribbean, setting your table as if you were there. For example, use a Mexican hat for the centre if you are serving Mexican food. You can even turn it upside down and fill it with bright florals.

For a Hawaiian theme, you might place silk leis on each chair or down the centre with lanterns. If you want a tropical theme, you might use vibrant colours or colours of the ocean, adding seashells on napkin rings down the centre or mixed with florals. See my Seashells and Flowers tabletop, where I have mixed seashells with silk florals.

Sources

My eyes are always wide open when scouting for interesting bits and pieces, and I'm always on the lookout for unique items or even second-hand gems. Below you'll find a list of places where I have found real treasures.

USA/CANADA

- Crate & Barrel
- Pottery Barn
- Pier 1 Imports
- West Elm
- Michaels
- Williams Sonoma

VANCOUVER AND LOWER MAINLAND

- Atkinson's
- Blooming Buds Florist
- Butter Baked Goods
- Cakes N Sweets
- Coquitlam Florist
- Elsa Corsi Jewellery
- Fino Lino Linens and Accesories
- Gilligan Girls Flowers on Main
- HomeSense
- Hudson's Bay Company
- Jamey McDonald Designs
- Just Essential Packaging
- Krause Berry Farms & Estate Winery
- Manuel Mendoza Couture
- Nadia Albano Style Inc.
- North Shore Linens
- One Stop Party Rentals
- Party Tailor Balloons
- Pedersen's Rentals
- Port Moody Flowers
- Rokko Sarees & Fabrics
- Salmon Party Rentals
- Sugar Vancouver
- The Bloomerie Florist
- The Pie Hole
- Thomas Hobbs Florist
- Trims
- Upright Design & Décor Rentals
- Valley Bakery

Recipe Credits

Recipe by Folco Gamberucci
- Pici or Bucatini with Pancetta — Image courtesy of pxhere.com

Recipes from *Toscana Mia: the Heart and Soul of Tuscan Cooking* by Umberto Menghi
- Stuffed Zucchini — Image courtesy of goodthymekitchen.com
- Tiramisu — Image courtesy of pxhere.com

Recipe by Maryann Nezis
- Roast Leg of Lamb — Image courtesy of taste.com.au

Recipe by Evangelia Kasdtrenakes
- Ravani — Image courtesy of khadizeskitchen.com

Recipes by chefs of Neyzen Travel & Yachting
- Karides Güveç — Image courtesy of tadindaseyahat.com
- Karnıyarık — Image courtesy of msarugula.wordpress.com

Recipe by the Beverly Hills Hotels and Bungalows
- McCarthy Salad — Image courtesy of la.eater.com

Recipes by The Poop Deck at Sandyport
- Johnny Cake — Image courtesy of meatsrootsandleaves.com
- Boiled Fish — Image courtesy of meatsrootsandleaves.com

Recipe by Compass Point Restaurant
- Conch Fritters — Image courtesy of roadfood.com

Recipe by Susan Hyatt
- Fried Plantain — Image courtesy of Susan Hyatt

Recipes by Tracy Flanagan
- Fish Cakes — Image courtesy of thymetoeat.ie
- Banana and Coconut Soup — Image courtesy of eggsandbanana.com

Photo Credits

All pictures in the book (including the front and back cover) were taken by Susan Hyatt, except the ones below.

Butter Studios

- Shades of White

Daniella Guzzo Photography

- Bahamian Rhapsody
- Greek Chic
- Susan Hyatt's photograph

Darla Furlani Photography

- All About Coral
- Anchors Aweigh
- Cocktails at the Bar
- Crisp Green and White
- Happy Hour
- Hibiscus and Bougainvillea
- Ladies who Lunch
- Leaves Everywhere
- Parrots and Tropical Leaves
- Splendour in the Summer
- Understated Elegance

Susan Hyatt has enjoyed making things beautiful since she was a child growing up in the Bahamas, where she was influenced by bright, bold colours and aesthetics. Susan spent more than two decades custom-designing dream weddings in Hawaii, Mexico, the Bahamas and Vancouver.

Her love for design and entertaining sparked the beginning of Tabletops by Susan. It all started with putting together beautiful tables at home for family and friends, but now Susan hopes to inspire everyone to be more creative with how they set their tables.

Susan enjoys working with clients at their homes, creating just the right tables for their special occasions or family gatherings. She also loves travelling with her husband Martin and spending time with her amazing children and grandchildren.

For more images of her stunning work, visit her website:

www.tabletopsbysusan.com